# Rethinking Higher Education

Thomas Lange
*Professor of Economics and Director of the
Centre for International Labour Market Studies,
Faculty of Management,
The Robert Gordon University, Aberdeen*

Published by the IEA Education and Training
Unit, 1998

First published in December 1998 by
The Institute of Economic Affairs
2 Lord North Street
Westminster
London SW1P 3LB

© IEA 1998

IEA Studies in Education No. 6
All rights reserved
ISBN 0-255 36421-0

Many IEA publications are translated into languages other than English or are reprinted. Permission to translate or to reprint should be sought from the General Director at the address above.

Printed in Great Britain by
Hartington Fine Arts, Lancing, West Sussex
Set in Century Schoolbook and Bookman Old Style

Contents

	Foreword	*Professor James Tooley*	5
	The Author		7
	Acknowledgements		7
1.	The Issue		9
2.	Supply to the Youth Labour Market		13
3.	Screening Britain's Graduates: Employers as Benefactors		18
4.	The Demand for Labour		22
5.	The Motivation for Higher Education		27
6.	Financing Higher Education: An Overview		32
7.	The Political Economy of Financing Higher Education		39
8.	Flexibility, Skills and Standards in Higher Education		42
9.	Lord Dearing's Response		47
10.	The Future of Higher Education in Britain		50

Figure 8.1: Trade-Off Between Entrance Requirements and Length of Study	45
Figure 8.2: Benefits and Costs of Screening	45

Table 2.1: Resident Population Aged 16-19 Compared with the Total Civilian Labour Force: Estimates and Projections, Great Britain, 1971-2006	14
Table 2.2: Female Activity Rates and Population Data by Age: Great Britain, 1971-2006	14

Table 2.3: Male Activity Rates and Population Data by Age: Great Britain, 1971-2006	15
Table 2.4: Participation in Higher Education in Britain, 1972-1995	17
Table 3.1: Early Findings on Rates of Returns to Education in Developed Economies	20
Table 4.1: Changes in the Demand for Labour, Great Britain, 1981-91 and Forecast for 1991-2000	23
Table 4.2: 'Dominant' Business Recruiters: Recruitment Factors in 1996	26
Table 5.1: First Destinations of UK Domiciled Men and Women Obtaining First Degrees, by Selected Subject of Study, 1994-95	30

References	53
Summary	**Back Cover**

Foreword

A consequence of the recent expansion of higher education has been in the news as I write this Foreword. One of the *very* new universities – Thames Valley University, which just managed to become a polytechnic in time to be created a university by government fiat in 1992 – has been damned by inspectors for the quality of its courses and teaching. The Vice-Chancellor has resigned and Sir William Taylor brought in to sort out the mess. Thames Valley University had noble aims – it wanted to extend access to those otherwise denied a higher education, and created courses and modules which would be popular and accessible. But in pursuing these aims to what might be seen as their logical conclusion – with the media latching on to everything from pop music to Indian cookery – the case raises one of the fundamental questions with which Professor Lange is concerned in this monograph: are we in Britain trying to provide too much higher education? And the concomitant question is: are the current funding mechanisms fair and efficient for students?

In this tightly argued paper, Lange suggests that the answer to the first question is likely to be in the affirmative, and to the second, negative. He suggests that government may have sacrificed the quality of higher education with its concern to raise numbers – and that there is no convincing economic argument to back this expansion. Significantly, he suggests that the current funding mechanisms – even with the relatively minor student contributions introduced by the government – undermine equity. Higher education is still 'a middle class scam', with the relatively less affluent subsidising the education of the middle classes. Current mechanisms also, of course, allow students the odd luxury of being able to make important life decisions without regard to economic considerations. This, argues Lange, can have serious social disbenefits, an expansion of higher education fuelled by artificial demand, leading to rampant credentialism and unemployable graduates.

His argument addresses concerns from a variety of literatures. He analyses the youth labour market and demand for highly skilled labour. He debates the 'screening hypothesis' versus human capital theory, and explores social and private rates of return to higher education, and their implications. Finally, he puts the whole argument in the context of public choice theory, pointing to various groups whose interests lie in the expansion of higher education, free at the point of delivery.

One of Lange's solutions to the problem of deteriorating quality in higher education is market-driven: income-contingent loans for students combined with realistic tuition fees charged by universities. The idea of income-contingent loans in this country can be traced back to a 1964 paper by Alan Peacock and Jack Wiseman, *Education for Democrats*, published by the Institute of Economic Affairs. For Peacock and Wiseman, such loans would better satisfy equality of opportunity than other funding proposals, but without sacrificing efficiency. Their proposals 'would minimise the financial obstacles facing talented students, and ...would significantly reduce the discriminations apparent in the present British system'. Lange seems to concur with this conclusion entirely.

Lange's work is a powerful contribution to this continuing important debate. I warmly welcome his work to the Studies in Education Series. As with all IEA publications, the paper represents the views of the author, not of the Institute (which has no corporate view), its Trustees, Advisers or Directors.

December 1998   JAMES TOOLEY
Director, IEA Education and Training Unit
Professor of Education, University of Newcastle-upon-Tyne

The Author

Thomas Lange is Professor of Economics and Director of the Centre for International Labour Market Studies (CILMS) at The Robert Gordon University, Aberdeen. He holds various honorary fellowships and professorships at universities and research institutions in Denmark, Germany and Sweden and has recently been appointed to the post of Contract Professor of Managerial Economics at the Polytechnic University of Bucharest, Romania. Prior to these appointments he was a Research Fellow at the Institute for Employment Studies (at the University of Sussex) and worked as a researcher and lecturer at the Universities of Westminster and Saarland (Germany).

Professor Lange has published over 50 articles and book contributions on economic policy, industrial relations and labour market analysis. Recent book publications include *The Economics of German Unification* (with Geoff Pugh, Edward Elgar Publishing, Aldershot), *Unemployment in Theory and Practice* (Edward Elgar Publishing, Aldershot), and *Understanding the School-to-Work Transition: An International Perspective* (Nova Science Publishers, New York).

Acknowledgements

I would like to thank my colleagues Keith Maguire and Geoff Pugh, James Tooley, the audience of my IEA Occasional Lecture on 11 March 1997 in London and two anonymous referees for their valuable comments and suggestions. I am grateful to J.R. ('Len') Shackleton for his general encouragement of my work on education and training policy in recent years. I also owe considerable thanks to my students at The Robert Gordon University whose lively discussions and debates on the topic have helped improve some of my arguments. The usual disclaimer applies. The views expressed are those of the author alone and do not necessarily reflect the opinion of members of staff at The Robert Gordon University or associates of CILMS which does not hold a corporate view.

T.L.

1 | The Issue

Higher education in Britain is changing, both quantitatively and qualitatively. The days when universities were seen primarily as promising testbeds for traditional classical scholarship are numbered. Higher education has become a £10 billion business and private sector involvement has grown in importance.[1] A rapid rise in the number of students has coincided with a slower increase in the number of institutions and a significant decline in financial resources per student. Although in Britain higher education accounts for a fifth of the total education budget, spending per student has plummeted in recent years from over £6,500 in 1989/90 to less than £4,500 in 1996/97. This, however, comes as no surprise. 'The central fact of British higher education is that in 1950 we had an elite participation rate of 5 per cent; today we face a mass system of higher education. As recently as 1989 Britain had the smallest higher education sector of any industrialised country. Today the participation rate in higher education has risen to a staggering 30 per cent' (British Broadcasting Corporation, 1996). In other words, one in three young people now enter higher education (compared with one in six in 1989).

Throughout this period, the majority of full-time undergraduate students resident in the UK or other EC

---

[1] An increasing share of off-the-job training activities, particularly for medium-sized and large companies, is carried out by higher education (HE) institutions. More than a third of all employers involved in the 1996 Skill Needs in Britain Survey, for example, contacted universities and HE institutions to discuss potential collaborations on skill developments. Only 28 per cent contacted other employers, 23 per cent discussed skill issues with employment bodies and a mere 8 per cent met with education/business partnerships to exchange views on longer-term skill needs. In fact, when asked which organisation had actually helped the employers in reaching their longer-term skill needs, with 78 per cent universities and HE colleges received the highest positive response (Skills and Enterprise Network, 1997).

countries received their higher education tuition free of charge.[2] The expansion of higher education has been financed largely by overloading the existing infrastructure, despite the large number of newly founded universities.[3] The discrepancy between increased enrolment, a slower expansion in the institutional framework and a real decline in actual expenditures devoted to higher education has led to talks about a financial crisis in higher education. Moreover, Britain's graduate skilling does not seem to meet the demands of business and industry (Institute of Employment Studies, 1996) and an increasing share of graduates end up in unemployment or underemployment. There appear to be growing concerns about the quality of higher education courses, culminating in the long-standing question of whether students may not be better off by acquiring those vital job skills on-the-job (Psacharopoulos, 1987). Can the delivery of relevant skills at higher education institutions be secured and improved? Does the system of higher education become a burden rather than a benefit for society? Can the system cope with ongoing expansion?

As recently as 200 years ago in Britain, it would have been perfectly easy to predict the life experiences of the next generation: barring war or crop failure, they would be virtually identical to those of their parents. The coming of industrialisation, the market economy which developed from it, and the assertion of new social relationships, began a quickening process of social and economic change which continues to accelerate. As a result, it would be foolish to pretend that it is possible to 'predict' how the youth labour market in Britain will develop. Just some decades ago, who would have predicted those factors which subsequently have so influenced the character of our current working lives: the

---

[2] Part-time students have to pay a fee which covers around 25 per cent of the costs of the course, as do postgraduate students. Equally, in further education most students aged 18 or above have to pay a fee which covers roughly a quarter of the costs of the course (DfEE, 1997).

[3] At present, the sector comprises over 180 higher education institutions, of which 100 are universities. In addition, nearly 100,000 students study for higher education qualifications at colleges of further education and increasing links are being developed between institutions in further and higher education (for further details see Rawlinson, Frost and Walsh, 1996).

IT revolution, the decline of manufacturing industry, the rise of the Pacific Rim economies, the convergence of European states, the explosion of female employment, the move from corporatism to state abstention, and so on? This unpredictability has profound consequences for government involvement in higher education, as explained below.

Young labour is after all only a collective term for a very substantial part of the population with domestic responsibilities and duties, ambitions and aspirations, likes and dislikes. The supply of it is not simply a matter of the allocation of an inanimate resource without opinions. The demand for labour has to take account of human strengths and weaknesses, and reflect society's view of the appropriateness of the tasks that may be given to young workers. In other words, only the purest of theoretical economists can hope to live out the assumption that labour of any age is a resource for productive purposes like any other resource. Moreover, ambitions, aspirations and motivations are changing over time.

However, those problems need not be a disastrous limitation on the usefulness of both a current stocktaking and a forward look. The circumstances of future youngsters will not be simply a reflection of the conditions at that time, but will rather be a cumulative consequence of developments between now and then. Thus, it is likely that much of any young person's experience of, and requirements for, higher education will be determined by factors which are closer to our own time, and within the ambit of our existing knowledge.

What needs to be borne in mind, however, is the changing relationship between higher education and the labour market. In the past, it was considered possible for educationalists to produce professionally qualified students in proportion to the projected needs of each profession (Siegel, 1967).

However, as Orivel (1996) puts it:

> 'These exercises almost always ended in failure, producing virtually systematic errors in prediction. The most important lesson learned from this failure concerned the very organisation of educational systems: educational systems must give up on the idea of producing a mass of future employees who are extremely narrowly specialised, unable to adapt to the evolution of labour markets and technologies.'

Instead, the skills of future employees must be fluid, convertible, adaptable; the very concept of 'profession' or 'occupation' in the narrow sense needs to be rethought. Most importantly, however, universities and higher education colleges must be prepared for education of a different kind: demand-oriented and customer-driven. But this raises the crucial issue that it must be associated with a market price, which in turn raises the important question on which we reflect here: who should pay the price? Should higher education be subsidised by the taxpayer or should funding be substantially private?

This brief survey discusses some findings on the readiness of young individuals to work and study, addresses the controversial issue of self-finance and tuition fees, and looks at how business needs are likely to change over time and at how these changes may be reflected in the size, character and function of higher education in Britain.

2 | Supply to the Youth Labour Market

We first undertake a basic analysis of the supply to the youth labour market in Britain as a point of departure. The demographic structure of a country has a strong influence on its economic success or failure. Labour is of undoubted importance in the economy, in both absolute and relative terms. As noted by Deakin (1996):

> 'The UK ranks fourth of the Group of Seven countries in the proportion of young people under age 15 of the total population. The UK proportions, for both males and females, in this age group are below the Group of Seven averages, ... but they are higher than the averages for the EEC. In respect of the relative size of the youth cohort, the UK has no great potential advantage over its competitors, nor has it a marked disadvantage – it is close to the average position.'

Demographic change is one variable to be considered but economic activity rates and the willingness to undertake further and higher study are of at least equal importance. The civilian labour force includes people aged 16 or over, who are either in employment or ILO unemployed.[4] Table 2.1 provides an overview of past, present and estimated future supply of youngsters as a proportion of the total civilian labour force.

The trends depicted in Tables 2.2–2.4 show that on balance activity rates[5] among younger people have fallen somewhat, reflecting a tendency to stay on in further and higher education.

---

[4] The ILO (International Labour Organisation) defines the unemployed as those people without a job who were available to start work within two weeks and had either looked for work in the previous four weeks or were waiting to start a job they had already obtained.

[5] The civilian activity rate in a given age/sex category is the civilian labour force expressed as a percentage of the population in that category, that is, the proportion of the population in work or actively seeking work.

Table 2.1: Resident Population Aged 16-19 Compared with the Total Civilian Labour Force: Estimates and Projections, Great Britain, 1971-2006

Year	Population aged 16–19: youth labour cohort (000s)	Total civilian labour force (000s)	Youth population cohort as % of total civilian labour force
Estimates			
1971	2,975	23,631	12.6
1980	3,613	25,446	14.2
1985	3,519	26,116	13.5
1990	3,069	27,415	11.2
1995	2,590	26,936	9.6
Projections			
1997	2,746	27,362	10.0
2000	2,806	27,701	10.1
2006	3,004	28,306	10.6

Source: Ellison *et al.* (1997).

Table 2.2: Female Activity Rates and Population Data By Age (thousands and percentages): Great Britain, 1971-2006

Age		1971	1981	1991	2001	2002
16-19	Popl.	1,457	1,797	1,419	1,379	1,394
	R (%)	65.0	66.7	69.7	60.7	60.4
	ALF	947	1,199	989	837	842
20-24	Popl.	2,062	2,052	2,105	1,678	1,716
	R (%)	60.2	70.7	73.9	72.1	72.4
	ALF	1,241	1,451	1,556	1,210	1,242

Age		2003	2004	2005	2006
16-19	Popl.	1,413	1,444	1,456	1,468
	R (%)	60.0	59.7	59.6	59.5
	ALF	848	862	868	874
20-24	Popl.	1,748	1,754	1,760	1,769
	R (%)	72.6	72.7	72.8	72.9
	ALF	1,269	1,275	1,281	1,290

Source: Ellison *et al.* (1997). Key: Popl. = resident population, R = civilian activity rate, ALF = active labour force.

Table 2.3: Male Activity Rates and Population Data By Age (thousands and percentages): Great Britain, 1971-2006

Age		1971	1981	1991	2001	2002
16-19	Popl.	1,518	1,882	1,496	1,443	1,460
	R (%)	69.4	69.4	72.6	66.5	66.4
	ALF	1,054	1,306	1,086	960	969
20-24	Popl.	2,099	2,107	2,184	1,740	1,777
	R (%)	87.7	86.8	88.2	81.9	82.0
	ALF	1,841	1,829	1,926	1,425	1,457

Age		2003	2004	2005	2006
16-19	Popl.	1,478	1,512	1,525	1,536
	R (%)	66.1	66.1	66.3	66.5
	ALF	977	999	1.011	1,021
20-24	Popl.	1,810	1,813	1,819	1,830
	R (%)	82.0	82.2	82.1	82.1
	ALF	1,484	1,490	1,493	1,502

Source: Ellison *et al.* (1997). Key: Popl. = resident population, R = civilian activity rate, ALF = active labour force.

During the 1980s and early 1990s, however, the number of young people fell markedly, producing the so-called 'demographic time bomb', whose explosion was so muted by severe recession. By the millennium that slim cohort of youth will have aged somewhat to give an equally slim cohort of individuals from whom (post)graduate students are classically drawn. It is thus possible that the increased willingness to study at the advanced level (see Table 2.4) will be more than offset by a shrunken stock of youngsters unless institutes of further and higher education are able to produce high-quality 'products' for a potentially decreasing stock of 'customers'. This argument will grow stronger as increasingly fewer graduates end up in jobs which require the type of skills they have acquired during their period of study (Institute for Employment Studies, 1996). In fact, overall growth in student numbers has slowed already and the demand for higher education has flattened out, especially at the first-degree level.[6] Is this yet another reason why expansion of higher

---

[6] At present, Britain has over 1.5 million students, over 50 per cent more

education needs to be promoted? Certainly, some commentators attribute this decline to government financial constraints (La Valle, Jagger, Connor and Rawlinson, 1996) rather than to course quality or demographic factors alone. As Kingston (1997) puts it:

> 'As the economy improves, but the cost of going to university rises, potential applicants are likely to be taking a more hard-headed monetary approach.'

Nevertheless, throughout the 1980s and early/mid-1990s an increased interest in further and higher education was clearly visible. This willingness to stay on in further and higher education may have a number of potential reasons. A popular argument is that growing demand for degree courses simply reflects the increasing demand for highly skilled personnel. There have indeed been a number of dramatic changes away from manual, low-skilled jobs to high-tech, high-skill positions. However, research into the question of how ability, cognitive skills and years of schooling affect earnings has shed light on another controversial issue: whether the level of education influences productivity at all and the effect is reflected in earnings, or whether it merely identifies workers with superior ability and personal attributes (Griliches and Mason, 1972). This view has been formalised in the 'screening hypothesis' which argues that advanced education is associated with increased productivity, but does not cause it. An alternative view suggests, however, that behind the increase in student numbers lies a conscious decision of youngsters, reflecting only in part the change in occupational structures. As employment for life and job security have become things of the past, the attempt to avoid youth unemployment, at least temporarily, can also be presented as an explanation for rising participation rates in advanced study courses.

Section 3 addresses the screening hypothesis and related

---

than in 1988/89. By the year 2000 the Open University expects to have 200,000 students registered in its distance education courses (compared with around 100,000 at present). However, between 1994/95 and 1995/96 the number of first degree full-time students enrolled at HE institutions is estimated to have grown by only 3 per cent. (La Valle, Jagger, Connor and Rawlinson, 1996.)

Table 2.4: Participation in Higher Education in Britain, 1972–1995

	1972	*1982*	*1991*	*1992*	*1994*	*1995*
Age participation rate %	7	13	19	23	30	31
Students in full-time higher education (thousands)	473.5	555.0	747.0	845.0	1,064.0	1,143.0
Students in part-time higher education (thousands)	174.2	300.0	428.0	455.0	515.0	558.0
Full-time teaching and research staff at universities (thousands)	29.7	33.7	31.9	32.6	34.5	n.a.
Ratio full-time students/full-time staff	15.9	16.5	23.4	25.9	30.8	n.a.

Source: National Statistics WebPage <www.ons.gov.uk>; own calculations.
n.a. = not available

matters.[7] An investigation of the demand side of the British labour market (Section 4) may help to shed some light on the issue of whether higher education is used as an escape route by youngsters faced with the prospect of unemployment.

---

[7] For a survey of contributions to the screening hypothesis, see Blaug (1985).

3 | Screening Britain's Graduates: Employers as Benefactors

It cannot be taken for granted that the primary result of courses in higher education is to augment the human capital stock. From another perspective their effects are best understood by concentrating on education's *signalling* function (Hamilton and Roesner, 1972; Spence, 1973; Taubman and Wales, 1974; Stiglitz, 1975). Traditional higher education is unlikely to provide the mix of specific skills required by employers as a proxy for inherent abilities, diligence and other not easily observable personal characteristics which help determine the employability of workers. Thus higher education has a sorting (or screening) function for employers faced with an excess of job applicants. Successful students may move a few places up the queue for future jobs. In fact, critics of the concept of human capital have argued that education may identify productive capacities without necessarily enhancing them (Arrow, 1973; Riley, 1979; Albrecht, 1981).[8] In this case it is possible that the public return to education will be driven below the private return. Against this background, one is tempted to question the value of higher education altogether. However, the screening hypothesis is not as damaging as it first appears to be. If education does not directly improve skills and productivity, then it may still be a profitable private investment, though society derives less benefit from it than is usually claimed. In other words, higher education may simply confer 'credentials'

---

[8] In principle there is nothing wrong with employers using education as a screening device. Employers need to use selection criteria when hiring workers, and it is both more efficient and equitable for education to be used as a criterion rather than race, religion or social background. However, if as some have argued higher education is open only to the economically better off in society, then some critics view the acceptance of education as a screening device as a means for 'legitimising the intergenerational transfer of inequality' (Bowles and Gintis, 1975).

that employers can use to select workers and to determine relative wages and salaries.

However, Joseph Stiglitz (1975) reminds us that

> 'economies with imperfect information with respect to qualities of individuals differ in fundamental ways from economies with perfect information. There may be, for instance, multiple equilibria in which one of the equilibria is Pareto inferior to another; the Pareto inferior equilibrium may involve either too much or too little screening, or it may entail the wrong kind of screening.'[9]

In any case, the crucial lesson that emerges from this is that there is another major benefactor of higher education – the employer. However, it may be that the latter does not need the skills directly imparted by higher education but rather values the attitudes and abilities normally associated with higher education, including the social and communication skills. So far, these skills have been only indirectly fostered by higher education, although it is increasingly recognised that some employers value them as highly as specific cognitive knowledge.[10] At the individual level, students still benefit from higher education. As far as society's benefits are concerned, however, the case is not clear-cut. Although there is little dispute that there are some beneficial effects on society of any form of education, the real question is whether social rates of return to education exceed private rates of return, thus justifying primarily public finance of courses, fees and related expenditures. In the early 1970s, the first attempts were made to carry out a comprehensive international comparison of the rate of return to investment in education (Psacharopoulos, 1973). Private and social rates of return to secondary and higher education were compared in 32 developed and developing countries. Some of these calculations were based on inadequate data and the exercise was repeated in the early 1980s as part of a World Bank Development Report (Psacharopoulos, 1981). This new comparison (see selected results in Table 3.1) reinforced the

---

[9] Pareto efficiency refers to the situation where it is impossible to make someone better off without making someone else worse off.

[10] Recent survey evidence suggests that cognitive knowledge is rated second to so-called *transferable 'core' skills* (see Section 4 for further details).

Table 3.1: Early Findings on Rates of Returns to Education in Developed Economies

Economy	Rate of Return by Educational Level %			
	Private		Social	
	Secondary	Higher	Secondary	Higher
Australia	14.0	13.9	n.a.	n.a.
Belgium	21.2	8.7	17.1	6.7
Canada	16.3	19.7	11.7	14.0
Denmark	n.a.	10.0	n.a.	7.8
France	13.8	16.7	10.1	10.9
W. Germany	n.a.	4.6	n.a.	n.a.
Italy	17.3	18.3	n.a.	n.a.
Japan	5.9	8.1	4.6	6.4
Netherlands	8.5	10.4	5.2	5.5
New Zealand	20.0	14.7	19.4	13.2
Norway	7.4	7.7	7.2	7.5
Sweden	n.a.	10.3	10.5	9.2
UK	11.7	9.6	3.6	8.2
US	18.8	15.4	10.9	10.9

Source: Psacharopoulos (1981)
n.a. = not available

concerns about public finance of higher education in its findings that

- the rate of return is higher in developing countries than in developed countries;
- the returns to primary education (whether social or private) are highest among all educational levels;
- the private returns to education are in excess of social returns, especially at the university level.

In other words, the comparison between private and social returns to education across a number of countries seems to reveal that the case for public funding of education in general and higher education in particular is considerably weaker than the public is led to believe.[11] The evidence suggests that even a considerable shift of the cost burden from the state to individuals, families and the private sector should not be regarded as a disincentive to investing in higher education, given the high private margin of profitability. Section 5 will revisit these issues and examine them in more detail.

---

[11] A more recent study about private returns to higher education in Britain estimated that for males the overall private return is 7 per cent and for females 5.8 per cent. According to this study, however, the rates of return vary significantly if the effects of social class are taken into account. For example, for males with unskilled, manual background private rates of return to higher education amount to a staggering 25 per cent, whereas their counterparts with a professional, managerial background receive a return of only 4 per cent (see Bennet, Glennerster and Nevison, 1992). However, it should also be emphasised that the reliability of estimates of rates of returns to education has frequently been questioned. Those commentators who favour public sector finance of higher education have argued that for reasons of upward bias in survey estimates, it would be unlikely for social returns to education to appear in double figures. In a similar vein, they argue that private returns are probably easy to exaggerate (see Weale, 1993).

4 | The Demand for Labour

The increased demand for highly skilled labour in professional and managerial occupations and the changing structure of British employment are frequently held responsible for both rising unemployment *and* increasing demand for places in further and higher education. It is accordingly these factors on which I now focus.

Since the early 1950s, the number of non-manual jobs has risen steadily and there are signs of a tendency to convergence in all the advanced industrial economies towards a situation in which, on average, non-manual labour accounts for between one-third and one-half of total employment. Between 1951 and 1971, the share of non-manual labour rose from one-quarter to nearly one-third of total employment in Britain. Since then, the share of non-manual jobs has risen continuously. By the early 1990s, employees in service industries accounted for about three-quarters of all employees in employment. If one adds to this the growing number of self-employed in the service sector, the decline in British manufacturing and production industries becomes apparent. For the next few years, some forecasts suggest a strong continuing increase in the numbers in scientific, engineering, technical, managerial, entrepreneurial and other professional occupations, with smaller increases in office and personal services and in skilled manual occupations. In contrast, the numbers of manual and low-skilled jobs are expected to decline even further, though at a lower rate than during the 1970s and 1980s (Pearson *et al.*, 1989), as Table 4.1 illustrates.

There is, indeed, not only a shift from manual to non-manual, but also a shift from unskilled to skilled occupations. As a consequence, higher standards of previous schooling and advanced education will become increasingly important. There is already a demand for a general upgrading of skills at intermediate and lower levels, and British companies are

Table 4.1: Changes in the Demand for Labour: Great Britain, 1981-91 and Forecast for 1991-2000

Occupation	Average change p.a.		No. in occupations, 1991 (millions)
	Actual 1981-91 (000s)	Forecast 1991-2000 (000s)	
Corporate managers and administrators	+52	+66	2.2
Managers/proprietors in agriculture and services	+24	+21	1.6
Science and engineering professionals	+17	+17	0.6
Health professionals	+4	+3	0.2
Teaching professionals	+19	+2	1.2
Other professionals	+23	+32	0.6
Science and engineering associate professionals	+10	+12	0.6
Health associate professionals	+9	+6	0.7
Other associate professionals	+35	+29	1.1
Clerical occupations	+9	−8	3.0
Secretarial occupations	+3	−10	1.1
Skilled construction trades	+6	−1	0.6
Skilled engineering trades	−20	−14	1.1
Other skilled trades	−32	−42	1.9
Protective services	+3	+3	0.3
Personal services	+26	+20	1.6
Buyers, brokers and sales representatives	+4	+1	0.5
Other sales	+20	+14	1.4
Industrial plant and machine operatives	−32	−42	1.6
Drivers and mobile machine operatives	−13	−7	0.8
Other agricultural etc.	−4	−4	0.2
Other elementary	−25	−35	2.4
All occupations	+137	+62	25.3

Source: Institute for Employment Research (IER).

expressing their interest in larger pay offers to groups of workers who are meant to fill so-called 'hard-to-fill' vacancies. Moreover, it has been argued that 'there seems every likelihood that these existing trends will continue and be further stimulated by factors likely to be of increasing importance in the next two decades: greater emphasis on quality and the wider use of new technologies' (PSI, 1991). It is, of course, true that modern technology has taken over a lot of tasks that previously fell to manual workers, and it is also true that our hopes of a rising standard of living are largely dependent on improved machinery, equipment and the use of information technology. These tendencies are also reflected in the market for graduates. The initiating force for all these changes is, however, the human brain. There are many problems to be sorted out in integrating the new technologies into the production process and adapting the labour force to them, but the primacy of human labour as the motivating agent remains unquestioned.

Over the past few decades the notion of 'employability' has become more relevant and the educational requirements of Britain's graduates have changed considerably. In the 1950s and 1960s recruiters of graduates were satisfied with students enrolling and undertaking courses in subject-oriented, classical scholarship, partly because of the university's role of educating the chosen few. One is reminded of the Humboldt model in Germany,[12] intended to be a model for the intellectual and character formation of an elite and that elite's training for higher status occupations. However, changes in the social structure of higher education closely paralleled the change in its societal function. This process can be traced back to the 19th century. As economies industrialised, higher education institutions became more diversified and differentiated.[13] As Ash (1996) puts it:

> '[one of the major issues] ... is nicely summarised by the conjunction of two terms often used in German but hard to translate into English: *'Bildung und Ausbildung'*. This refers to the dichotomy – some call it a contradiction – between the claim

---

[12] For further details about the early ideals of higher education in Germany see McClelland (1980).

[13] This was achieved not so much by transforming or reforming existing institutions, but by adding new types of institutions.

that higher education serves a higher purpose, ...and the more strictly practical claim that education is professional training. This tension has been and will continue to be central to the history of higher education throughout the developed world'.

What is undeniable, however, is that today employers' requirements are more varied and include demands for characteristics such as work experience, the ability to work in a team and personal skills.[14] A recent study undertaken by PIP (1996), a statistical service for higher education, found that these skills were considered to be of considerable importance when it comes to employers' hiring decisions, particularly amongst business recruiters. PIP's national survey has shown that 89 per cent of all dominant business recruiters mentioned 'work experience' and 85 per cent 'personal skills' as important recruitment factors. Relevant course content, however, was mentioned by only 65 per cent of respondents. Cognitive knowledge seems to be of relatively little importance; by contrast, so-called 'transferable' or 'core skills' seem to have moved to the top of the business agenda (Table 4.2).

The importance attributed to communication and presentation skills of degree-qualified individuals, however, is only half of the story. Employers are likely to use other personal characteristics as well as, or instead of, work experience and educational credentials when hiring decisions are being made (Phelps, 1972). In many developed countries it is, in principle illegal to use such characteristics as gender, ethnic status or age as a means of allocating scarce jobs; in practice, legislation is often ineffective. To the extent that employers accord importance to such characteristics as gender and ethic status, education will be less effective as a means of improving employment prospects of graduates.

Notwithstanding these problems, however, we may work on the assumption that the limitations of higher education are properly understood and proper action is taken to incorporate,

---

14 In other words, as salaries for graduates increase employers seem to make sure that they get 'value for money'. Between 1994 and 1995, graduate starting salaries have risen by 6 per cent, ahead of the increase in median earnings. In 1995, 69 per cent of new graduates received starting salaries ranging from £13,000 to £15,999. A significant proportion (12 per cent) earned over £17,000 (La Valle, Jagger, Connor and Rawlinson, 1996).

Table 4.2: 'Dominant' Business Recruiters: Recruitment Factors in 1996

Recruitment Factors	Proportion of Employers Who Named Characteristics as Being Of Relevance (%)
Work experience	89
Personal skills	85
Degree classification	81
A-levels	77
Course content	65
O-levels/GCSE	50
Teamworking	50
Computing skills	42

Source: PIP (1996).

whenever possible, elements of transferable skills in degree programmes. Are there any other reasons why an expansion of higher education may be an illogical and expensive exercise for individuals and society as a whole?

5 | The Motivation for Higher Education

Certainly additional higher education can be regarded, at least in part, as yielding consumption benefits, for example, as a means of acquiring positive utility for those directly involved in the process of gaining advanced knowledge. However, the main source of motivation to both suppliers and purchasers of higher education is likely to take the form of investment benefits. For colleges and universities this translates into an increase in revenues at a time when the system is encouraged to work more closely with business and industry and to scale down the reliance on government funding. The efforts to increase the number of postgraduate full-cost courses thus have some immediate financial appeal.

At the individual level, it is argued that a return on human capital investment may originate from a rightward shift in the marginal revenue product curve which raises the value of labour input to both the firm and (via higher rates of pay) the individual undertaking the education. Recent evidence suggests that the financial rewards of higher education can be substantial. A report by the Institute for Fiscal Studies found that men with first degrees on average earn about 15 per cent more than men without, and women with degrees get on average 35 per cent more than those without (Blundell et al., 1997). Such effects of higher education, however, are based on the crucial underlying assumption that the economy suffers from a shortage of graduates and that high-skill vacancies remain largely unfilled or go disproportionately to those individuals whose skill levels do not measure up to the actual job requirements. Equally, it is argued that additional investments in higher education may be seen as shifting the production possibility frontier for the economy to the right, that is, providing a platform for what is often referred to as sustainable growth.[15] Why else would the CBI like to see the participation rate in higher education increase to 40 per cent? The arguments sound attractive and appealing. Let's educate the nation; let's make Britain a better, more productive place. Unfortunately, the empirical evidence gathered to analyse graduates' employment destinations suggests some sobering thoughts. A recent study by the Policy Studies Institute estimated the short-term returns to obtaining a degree-level qualification and compared them with non-graduates who could have entered higher education (Lissenburgh and Bryson, 1996). The analysis shows that graduates who are economically active spend less time in paid work when they are aged 22 and 23 years than non-graduates. Even when the graduates' lack of previous labour market experience and their relatively recent commencement of job search is taken into account, obtaining a degree had only a broadly neutral effect on the amount of time spent in full-time work.

Even if graduates find full-time employment, a rather gloomy picture emerges. The Institute for Employment Studies' report entitled *What Do Graduates Really Do?* followed three cohorts of graduates from one university. A breathtaking level of 'underemployment' came to light. Three-fifths of graduates were doing tasks which required little skill or knowledge, and certainly not the skills acquired through their university studies. Moreover, as Tooley (1996) points out,

> 'one disturbing aspect of this report is that it contains nothing new. The 1990 government report 'Highly Qualified People: Supply and Demand', for example, showed that Britain already has considerably more in the way of highly qualified labour than it can absorb in any capacity. ... these reports more or less reiterate what the Robbins Report had said almost 30 years earlier – that even a fifth of scientists and technologists were 'in categories of employment in which it is unlikely they were making full use of their qualifications'.

What seems to have happened can be described as a transformation of modern society in which more and more

---

[15] Although there is ample evidence that education makes both a direct and an indirect contribution to economic growth, the chicken-and-egg relationship between education and growth can never be fully established. For a general discussion see Psacharopoulos and Woodhall (1991).

members of a given age group see universities not as a route to high-status occupations, but as the main means of gaining access to advanced educational credentials considered absolutely necessary to maintaining any reasonable standard of living. But how successful are Britain's youngsters in achieving these goals and which subjects do they pick to secure regular employment? An analysis of the labour market destination of students following their first degree is eye-opening (see Table 5.1). It will come as little surprise that business, technology, computing and IT related subjects have comparatively high employment rates (75 per cent, 69.4 per cent and 77.5 per cent, respectively). In employability terms, however, traditional degree courses such as those in natural sciences and the humanities fare considerably worse. Moreover, with over 30 per cent they also include the highest percentage of students undertaking further study, very often in business and management conversion courses. What is really disturbing is that, in all these subject areas, graduate unemployment (those neither in employment nor in further study/training) lies above 11 per cent. However, this is unlikely to rise further because many graduates will displace less qualified people. As La Valle, Jagger, Connor and Rawlinson (1996) put it:

> 'It is likely that the increasing supply of graduates during the rest of the decade will be greater than the rising employer demand for places, thus leading to a continuing excess of supply over demand for newly qualified graduates ... Some of this will amount to graduate under-utilisation, and lower than anticipated salary and job expectations amongst the graduates themselves. ... A degree does not guarantee a better job, or even any job, but it does give a distinct advantage in the labour market to most people in terms of opening up careers opportunities, better earnings and the lower likelihood of being unemployed, when graduates are compared with non-graduates.'

The last point made by La Valle *et al.* is crucial and it is discussed further in Section 8. What can already be said, however, is that at the individual level, the possession of a university degree is beneficial, as long as there is a large number of potential competitors for jobs in the labour market who do not possess the same formal credentials. As higher education continues to expand, however, this advantage will become less pronounced.

Table 5.1: First Destinations of UK Domiciled Men and Women Obtaining First Degrees, By Selected Subject of Study, 1994/95

Subject area	Employed (% of total)	Further study (% of total)	Not available for employment (% of total)	Seeking employment/ Training (% of total)	Total of known destinations
Biological and Veterinary Science	5,160 (52.1)	3,291 (33.2)	473 (4.8)	1,215 (12.3)	9,906 (100)
Physical and Mathematical Sciences	7,032 (50.8)	4,624 (33.4)	638 (4.6)	1,553 (11.2)	13,847 (100)
Computer Science	4,560 (77.5)	487 (8.3)	145 (2.5)	694 (11.8)	5,886 (100)
Engineering and Technology	9,446 (69.4)	2,055 (15.1)	485 (3.6)	1,627 (11.9)	13,613 (100)
Social, Economic and Political Studies	9,314 (61.2)	3,125 (20.5)	842 (5.5)	1,937 (12.7)	15,218 (100)
Business and Admin. Studies	12,687 (75.0)	1,399 (8.3)	798 (4.7)	2,024 (12.0)	16,908 (100)
Humanities	4,134 (51.3)	2,490 (30.9)	426 (5.3)	1,002 (12.4)	8,052 (100)

Source: Derived from Higher Education Statistics Agency (1996); the first destination target population includes all students obtaining relevant qualifications during the period 1 October 1994 to 31 July 1995 whose study was primarily full-time. The reference date for the first destinations was 31 December 1995. Institutions reported destinations of qualifiers which had been firmly established by this date and which took effect no later than 31 March 1996. Coverage of first destinations thus refers to a minimum of 5 months and a maximum of 18 months after the period of study had come to an end.
Note: Percentages may not sum up to totals because of rounding.

The type of labour force that our modern economies now need is both specialised and flexible. However, it does not necessarily follow that there is no room for simple jobs and unskilled workers, since this depends on the way in which labour supplements modern technology. Many simple tasks are very difficult to mechanise, or the unit of production or service is on too small a scale, or too diversified, to warrant the extensive use of capital equipment. In other words, there are only so many highly skilled graduates the economy can use. The emergence of business- and service-oriented economic sectors displacing heavy industry and manual blue-collar sectors pulled vast numbers of young people into a system of higher education which on grounds of current and likely future evidence is neither designed nor structured to receive them. As a consequence, the value added of an ever larger number of students[16] undertaking courses in higher education seems to become smaller, both for individuals and society as a whole.

---

[16] As mentioned in Section 2, over the next decade or so the total number of students is likely to fall; the proportion of young people who decide to enter higher education, however, may still increase.

6 | Financing Higher Education: An Overview

The question of expansion leads inevitably to the problem of finance. Who should be responsible for the bill of an ever-increasing number of courses, higher education institutions and students? Who should pay for higher education anyway? Even if the expansion of higher education should continue to receive what is, on the basis of the analysis thus far, *illogical* approval, it is by no means certain that any future government will be able to find substantial additional resources. At the present time, with the Labour government committed not to raise income taxes, the problem with increased tax funding is self-evident. The alternative would, of course, be to suggest what until recently remained unthinkable: the student picks up the bill. Indeed, strong support for this alternative can be found in studies which have shown that public subsidies for education *benefit the rich rather than the poor* (Hansen and Weisbrod, 1969; Pechman, 1970; Schultz, 1972; Jallade, 1973; Fields, 1974; Psacharopoulos, 1977; Blaug, 1982; Bowman, Millot and Schiefelbein, 1984; and Meesook, 1984). In other words, a policy of shifting more of the financial burden to private rather than public funds could be justified on grounds of social equity as well as economic efficiency. These results have been particularly marked in developing countries where it has been argued that 'public subsidies for higher education ... have the perverse effect of transferring income from poor taxpayers to rich families, whose children benefit from subsidised education' (Psacharopoulos and Woodhall, 1991).[17]

---

[17] Education subsidies involve intergenerational transfers of income as well as transfers between income groups. Ideally, of course, analysis should be concerned with the effects of both taxes and subsidies on lifetime, rather than cross-sectional earnings and income, but the necessary longitudinal data are not always available.

Revisiting recent history, the student support system in Britain appears rather generous. Until 1990 full-time UK-based undergraduate students received 100 per cent grants for maintenance, means tested according to parental income. The Conservative government in 1990 introduced loans[18] which have progressively replaced grants for living costs. However, tuition costs have been largely left unaltered (although an element of student contribution has been introduced under the Labour government – Section 9 below). Notwithstanding this, the opposition to self-financing is considerable and focuses largely on the fairness argument of having unlimited access to higher education. The problem with unlimited access is that it can harm the reputation of the system and diminish employment probabilities for individuals. Section 8 will deal with this argument more explicitly. In general terms, however, the quality issue can be discussed by reference to revenue requirements of higher education institutions. If falling numbers of students coincide with government spending cuts per student, then there would be a strong incentive to admit those students who are able to pay their own, full-cost tuition fees.[19] It is here that the story of self-finance will experience an unexpected U-turn.

At first sight, it appears that if admissions were based on the ability and willingness to pay, quality in higher education would fall. However, once a mechanism has been found to make students contribute to the costs of higher education, demand will find its own level without damaging the quality of courses.

If students were to be in a position where they had to pay fees out of their own or their parents' pockets they might think twice about entering the system for reasons unrelated to

---

[18] Better-off parents are expected to make a contribution of up to £2,000 a year to supplement the loan.

[19] It may be argued that it is particularly tempting to admit overseas students whose fees are considerably higher than those of their British counterparts. We have witnessed a dramatic growth in aggregate numbers of overseas students since the late 1980s, up by 40 per cent between 1988/89 and 1993/94. From the student's perspective, studying overseas has been encouraged by a number of EU exchange programmes. More than 50 per cent of all overseas entrants to full-time degree courses in 1993/94 were from other EU countries (Greenaway and Tuck, 1995).

the acquisition of skills (such as prolonging irresponsibility or avoiding youth unemployment). Those youngsters deterred from applying for admission are likely to be those who should not have been in higher education in the first place[20] – providing that there is equal access to student loans, as discussed below, to avoid potential accusations of unfair treatment of the economically less well off. In addition, those who decide to enter higher education after all will have an incentive to put considerable pressure on higher education institutions to ensure appropriate standards and 'high quality' programmes, that is, in the eyes of many employers, programmes which combine some elements of traditional academic excellence with a vocational mission.

This leaves the question of whether and how student loans should be provided and distributed. These questions are nothing new.[21] What appears to be of primary importance in Britain today has already been examined by a number of commentators some decades ago, both in Britain and elsewhere. As long ago as the 1970s, for example, the US House of Representatives Committee on Education and Labor commented that

> 'the student loan program is not an unmixed blessing, nor an entirely unmitigated evil ... In today's fiscal and educational policy circumstances, loans are needed. Our task is to improve the structure of the existing programs so as to maximise its service to students and minimise the possibility of abuse'. (Rice, 1977)

A number of studies has suggested that, at least for some groups of youngsters, the average rate of return to education

---

[20] As a result of encouraging only motivated youngsters to enter the system, quality assessments of higher education may also become considerably easier. Motivation is presumably an individual characteristic important to the quality of education offered to the student, yet not easily observable. If a 'mixed bag' of motivated and less motivated students, their marks and their labour market destinations were to be assessed, however, it would be difficult to attribute any concise merit to higher education alone. Put crudely, unless we can at least reduce the share of unmotivated students, a superior performance of a sub-group will not necessarily reflect an impact of the actual degree course but rather the better motivation among participating students.

[21] See West (1994) for a useful survey, and Peacock and Wiseman (1964).

is relatively low (see, for example, Bennett, Glennerster and Nevison, 1992). If these rates of return are still positive, however, and possibly higher than social rates of return, it does not follow that the government should pick up the total bill. Instead, it is desirable to introduce some elements of loan finance. This still leaves us with the question of what kind of loan scheme should be on offer. Should we stick to 'traditional' government loan schemes, based on a mortgage principle with repayments in fixed instalments over a fixed period? Should we revisit the proposal of a graduate tax? Or are there alternative mechanisms that can be deployed to make access to student loans open and fair?

Moreover, any discussion of equity implications must incorporate the question of whether it is possible to devise a scheme which will limit the danger of deterring very large numbers of youngsters. These and related questions have frequently been raised in the relevant literature and a number of policy proposals has been developed to address these issues. Some of the most widely acclaimed contributions to this discussion are from Nicholas Barr and his collaborators at the London School of Economics (Barr, 1991, 1993; Barr and Falkingham, 1993). In a series of papers they discuss a range of alternative ways to finance education and training activities in Britain. According to Barr and Falkingham (1993), the following principal three approaches can be distinguished:

1. Mortgage-type Loans

This scheme typically has repayment in fixed instalments over a fixed period. Two strategic problems with mortgage-type loans have been highlighted. First, 'students bear a much higher fraction of the risk, thus deterring applicants, particularly from lower socio-economic groups. This is inefficient because it wastes talent and is inequitable because it reduces intergenerational mobility'. Second, it is argued that this type of loan scheme 'creates problems with the supply of loans. Lending for educational purposes is risky, since there is no security. The resulting capital-market imperfection leads to a shortage of loan capital for educational investment'.

2. Graduate Tax

This would be a tax of, say, one per cent of taxable income below the national insurance upper earnings limit for all persons who have attended at least two years of post-18 education, with repayment continuing until a specific time (a certain age limit, for life or until retirement, for instance). Although a number of commentators has recently revisited the possibility of a graduate tax in Britain, Barr and Falkingham (1993) argue that 'with a loan, no one repays more than he/she has borrowed; with a graduate tax, higher earners repay more than they have borrowed'.

3. Income-Contingent Loan

Finally, it has been argued that the above problems can be largely avoided by introducing an income-contingent loan scheme, characterised by repayments of x per cent of the individual borrower's subsequent annual income.

Barr and Falkingham (1993) argue that income-contingent loans

> 'offer the borrower some protection against potential future poverty, thus minimising the impediment to access. A properly designed scheme can also help to mobilise funds from which students can borrow.'

In simulation models it has been shown by Barr and his collaborators that this scheme could save the British government up to £1 billion a year.[22] Similarly, West (1998) argues that the income-contingent loan scheme is the most efficient and fairest route to a student loan scheme.

However, by simply asking the student to cover the costs of higher education, does this ignore the benefits of higher education to society as a whole? If so, it might be thought justifiable to argue for a 'mixed economy' of combined loan and grant schemes. These have, indeed, been tried in a number of countries, most recently in Australia (Chapman,

---

[22] 'Assuming no earnings growth, the government loan scheme imposes heavy front-end costs, but collects no more in total repayments than the income-contingent loan scheme. If loans are offered to full-time and part-time students, 77 per cent of total lending is repaid under the government scheme and 81 per cent under the income-contingent scheme' (Barr and Falkingham, 1993).

1992) and Sweden (Morris, 1989). As suggested by Woodhall (1982):

> 'a combined loan and grant scheme recognises that both society and the individual student benefit from higher education. The grant and any interest subsidy on the loan, ensure that part of the cost is met by society as a whole, out of general taxation. The repayable loan ensures that the individual student also contributes to the cost, but only when he or she is able to afford it, that is, when enjoying the financial benefits of higher education'.

Two common arguments for some element of government subsidy are, *first*, that, even though it may be true that individual rates of returns exceed social rates of returns (see Table 3.1), higher education creates some positive externalities, for example, that individual A's education and training increases individual B's productivity (see Berger and Leigh, 1989, Cochrane, O'Hara and Leslie, 1980, Lucas, 1988, Rosenzweig, 1990, Weale, 1992, and Christoffersen, 1996). However, other commentators stress that there are negative externalities too, including 'social unrest among a highly educated, yet significantly unemployed, intelligentsia' (West 1995 p. 142), and the issue of 'qualification inflation' (Dore 1976, Seville and Tooley 1997). It may be hard to say whether there is any net social benefit when these are taken into account.

Second, Nicholas Barr (1993) identifies another potential benefit:

> 'Unless the extreme version of the screening hypothesis holds, higher education raises a student's earnings and, thereby, increases his/her future tax payments. In the absence of any subsidy, an individual's investment in a degree would confer a "dividend" on future taxpayers. This line of argument can be used to justify any type of investment which raises future income; that is precisely what usually happens through the tax system, at least so far as business investment is concerned. The "tax dividend" point gives an efficiency case for some subsidy, but it is not possible to show how much.'

This case would seem to be undermined by West's (1998) argument, that it would be unfair and inefficient to subsidise students because they will pay potentially higher taxes, since as is easy to demonstrate empirically, 'the ability to earn the extra income is *not* perfectly correlated with the receipt of higher education'. The inefficiency is demonstrated by comparing

> 'two individuals who are alike in all respects except that one obtains income-generating human capital via university training while the other reaches the same income level by undertaking substantial saving to get himself/herself, say, a grocer's business or by entering professional sports or entertainment. ... Since "grocers" will be subject to the same income tax rates as the university graduates, the incentive to enter the grocer businesses will be relatively discouraged. In other words there will be an allocative distortion: too little investment in grocer business relative to formal human capital investment.' (West, 1998, p. 28)

One could go on forever refining and detailing a foolproof system of private/public sector finance, which takes into account the respective merits of these types of arguments. However, what is important is to concede the principle, justified in terms of both sides of the argument, that students should contribute to the costs of higher education – whether in full or in part – and that universities are allowed to charge the appropriate fee. Such a system ensures that the major beneficiaries of higher education are held responsible for its finance. It also, crucially, could reintroduce an element of quality assurance without having to rely on public sector watchdogs.[23]

However, an alarmingly large number of colleagues, commentators and politicians appear to have chosen to adopt a different line of thought, with, it is argued, foreseeable consequences for higher education in Britain. Unfortunately, policy-makers acting in good faith, attempting to promote the public interest, seem unable to disentangle the complexity of higher education provision. Why is it then that higher education still is and continues to be financed largely by the public hand?

---

[23] See Seville and Tooley (1997) for discussion of the difficulties inherent in these public quality assurance mechanisms.

7 | The Political Economy of Financing Higher Education

Private funding of higher education would, of course, have some profound implications for a number of interest groups in society. Power in the political market-place is unevenly spread. The demand for policy intervention tends to be concentrated among producer groups with particular interests in common who are individually prepared to contribute to the cost of lobbying in expectation of increased surpluses and other income. On the supply side, politicians will tend to concede those policies which appear to offer the greatest political advantage in terms of securing or retaining power. At present, the financing of higher education figures prominently on the political agenda.

Public choice analysis has been applied to an increasing range of policy issues.[24] It can offer a plausible explanation of the pattern of government intervention and economic regulation in parliamentary democracies. The ostensible rationale for government policies is increasingly seen, in this framework, as only part of the picture – and it is looked on with some suspicion. It has been argued by some that there is a systematic tendency for oversupply of intervention – a genuine case of 'government failure' (Stigler, 1971). Are such arguments relevant in considering the financing of higher education?

Certainly, many interest groups stand to gain from government regulation and funding. Trade unions, for example, are typically strongly in favour of increased formal provision of education and training. Regulation and insistence on formal qualifications can be used to reduce competition in the labour market. Wherever possible, unions tend to press for

---

[24] James Buchanan, Gordon Tullock and Anthony Downs were early figures in this school. Seminal works include Downs (1957); Buchanan and Tullock (1962); Stigler (1971); and Buchanan *et al.* (1980).

higher entry qualifications to jobs, a policy enhancing 'rents'[25] to existing workers.

Employers also hope to gain from government funding in higher education. Public funding, as I have argued earlier, substitutes for vocationally oriented courses otherwise financed by students and/or employers themselves. It thus comes as no surprise that the UK's Confederation of British Industry supports the expansion of higher education up to, and above, 40 per cent of the working population. Similar targets are now government policy too.

Then there is the body of university lecturers who fear for their jobs if higher education becomes subject to market forces and quality competition. Academics, in their roles both as educators and researchers, have generally welcomed with open arms enhanced public investment in higher education. There appears to be a general willingness to trade off competition for job security, even if this means the opening up of higher education to markets previously deployed by further education colleges.

Finally, the attractiveness of intervention in higher education to politicians is easy to discern – particularly in recent years when higher unemployment has coincided with a loss of faith in demand management. The need to 'be seen to be caring about Britain's youngsters', which can be presented as improving long-term competitiveness as well as alleviating short-term problems, is a powerful one.

Therefore, in examining policies adopted towards higher education, we need to bear in mind the particular interests which interventionist behaviour may serve. To understand the refusal of some corners to open up higher education to a more flexible demand-led, privately financed system, it is essential to look carefully at the coalition of pressure groups united behind particular initiatives. It may be that some of the undesired results of government intervention in this area are under-emphasised by those promoting their own interests, rather than those of students and the economy as a whole.

However, it is not only the financing of higher education – the focal point of recent discussions – which needs to be addressed to reform the system of higher education in Britain. Another set of demands voiced by business and industry

---

[25] Returns in excess of the earnings which they could obtain elsewhere.

involves a greater degree of flexibility, in both length of study and course content. Amongst politicians too, the desired length of degree programmes has re-emerged as a central feature of discussions on different fee payments in Scotland for students from England, Wales and Northern Ireland. The controversial arrangements which exclude English, Welsh and Northern Irish students who choose to study at Scottish universities from fee exemptions in year four of their degree programmes have caused considerable unease amongst many commentators, analysts and members of the House of Lords who opposed the move on three consecutive occasions. The differential treatment in fee exemptions has also been claimed to be a government attempt to standardise the length of an undergraduate university degree to three years. A considerable political battle is fought over this issue, reinforced by references to Scottish devolution and new constitutional responsibilities. Irrespective of these discussions, however, one question has received relatively little attention: Does a uniform length of degree programme make any economic sense?

8 | Flexibility, Skills and Standards in Higher Education

We are apt nowadays to take it as axiomatic in our kind of education system that first university degrees have to take at least three years to complete.[26] Geoff Mason (1997), of the National Institute of Economic and Social Research (NIESR), however, has argued that

> 'most employers stress their needs for a good mix of university graduates and of intermediate-level personnel, with the latter acquiring skills and practical experience through employment-based training as well as classroom study in FE colleges. It would be agreeable simply to extend full-time university students' privileges to vocational education students but, if no new money is available for this purpose, then this gives added weight to proposals for university tuition fees... However, the imposition of such fees across all years of university study would ignore the overlap between further education – which needs to be expanded – and the early years of higher education.' (Mason, 1997, p. i)

Mason goes on to argue that the system of higher education needs to adjust to this overlap by developing new interim qualifications, similar to the two-year associates degrees in the United States. The primary objective of this exercise would be to shorten the length of study and to reduce the incentive to complete a full degree programme, which –

---

[26] Or four years in Scotland. This is, of course, still considerably shorter than most degree courses in continental Europe. At some universities in Germany, for example, the average period of study for a first degree in economics is twice as long as in Britain. At the University of Buckingham – arguably more aware of market pressures – to take a very different example, an undergraduate two-year course is already on offer, without arguably undermining the quality of the degree thus earned. Similar condensed courses are available through the for-profit higher education sector in the USA, again where suppliers are much more acutely aware of pressures from consumers (see Sperling and Tucker, 1997; Sperling, 1998).

according to Mason – has a relatively small pay-off in terms of post-degree rates of pay, employment and career opportunities. Even if such developments were thought desirable, however, there are a number of problems and uncertainties to overcome. Universities would be faced with such questions as 'What administrative changes do we have to initiate to cope with such developments?' and 'What financial and staffing implications does the new system bring about?'. Furthermore, if academic requirements fall short of the academic level of those students who complete a full degree programme, then it may become increasingly complex to cater for the differentiation in levels of subject knowledge and core skills at various exit points. The reliability of degrees as an appropriate screening mechanism for employers may also come into question.

As discussed earlier (see Section 3) in the screening model higher education is thought to play a major role in screening individuals for quality. It can be argued that entrance requirements need to be high for both two- and three-year degrees to ensure adequate precision of screening. Inadequate screening will be costly for both the student and the employer. In Arrow's screening model (1973), for example, we can detect two aspects, with each of which we can associate a cost. Universities set an entrance standard, S_0, and students then have to undergo a certain length of course, L, before being pronounced fit to graduate. Some commentators argue that the social cost[27] of setting a high entrance standard in higher education can be equated with 'wasted ability'. Mass education requires a low S_0. The costs associated with the length of study are then the foregone earnings of students. At first sight, this leads us to conclude that both the entrance requirements into higher education and the length of study should be low (to minimise social and private costs, respectively). However, so far we have ignored the benefits of higher education as a screening mechanism. As Siebert (1985, p. 56) puts it:

> 'In the screening approach the benefits of the education system are that it identifies pre-existing characteristics more or less precisely. Note that it is this precision, the expected quality of the graduate, which is important.'

---

[27] In the original article by Arrow (1973) these costs were ignored.

In other words, entrance standards and the length of study will influence both benefits and costs. Lower values of either variable presumably reduce the expected quality of the graduate, as demonstrated in Figures 8.1 and 8.2.

Figure 8.1 illustrates an assumed trade-off between entrance requirements and length of study for a given expected quality of a graduate, as indicated by the isoquant[28] EQ_2. An easier entrance policy ($Š_0$) implies that courses will take longer to achieve the same precision of certification. A shortened course length implies that entrance requirements need to be increased to remain on the same isoquant. Equally, it can be argued that if L remains unaltered and S_0 is falling, screening is likely to deliver less precision. In Figure 8.2, this is illustrated by a shift in the social benefits curve downwards.

We can, of course, move away from the *ceteris paribus* assumption and alter the course content in such a way that the delivery of skills required by employers will be given priority treatment. This would mean that the introduction of vocationally applicable modules combined with transferable skills could be used to compensate for either lower entrance requirements or a shortened study period. There is a natural limit to these changes in course curricula. And anyway, why should we aim for this kind of compensation when the proposed system could effectively be used both to comply with employers' demands and to raise the quality of graduates? This would mean that selection through self-finance would be complemented by selection through increased entrance requirements, thereby moving the graduate on to a higher-quality isoquant. Politically, such a system might be difficult to sell. Moreover, in the short run it might lead to a fall in student numbers and, at least temporarily, to a fall in university revenues. However, increased quality would make it easier to sell the product 'higher education' in the long run. Any educational entrepreneur acting rationally would seek to exclude students who would drag down the overall perform-

---

[28] If 'quality of graduate' is our end product, 'produced' by our inputs, entrance requirements and length of study, then an isoquant represents the various processes available for producing the quality of graduates in a technically efficient manner, *ceteris paribus*. A more efficient system for other reasons will cause the isoquants to move towards the origin (EQ_1).

Figure 8.1: Trade-Off Between Entrance Requirements and Length of Study

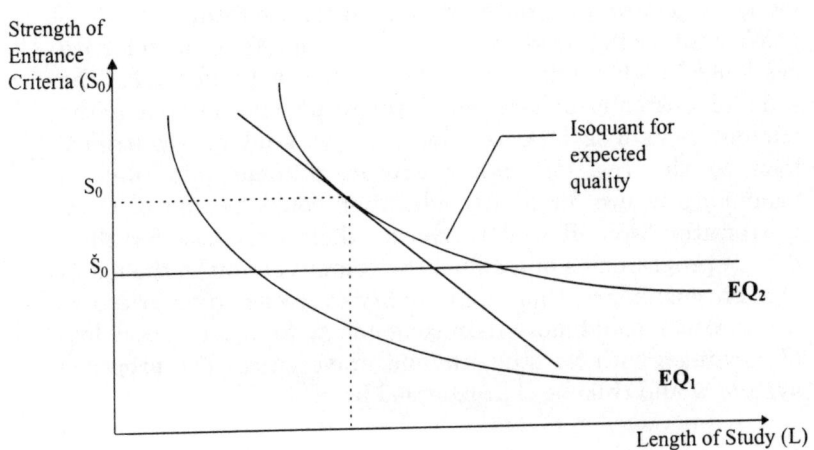

Source: Siebert (1985)

Figure 8.2: Benefits and Costs of Screening

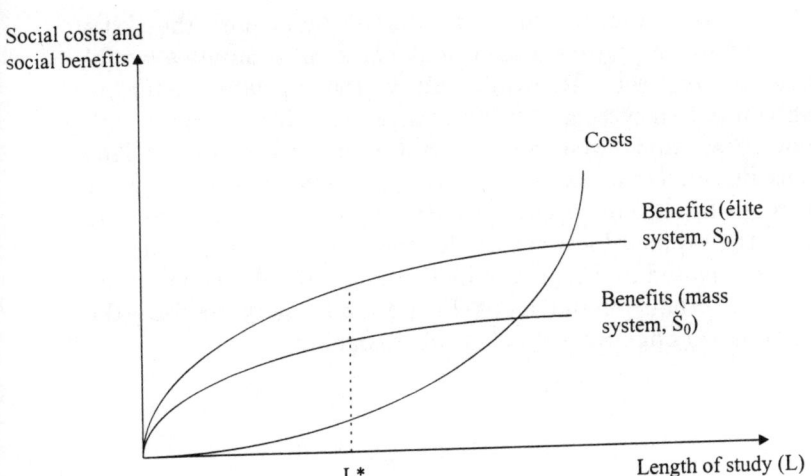

Source: Siebert (1985)

ance of the degree, its major selling point to parents and employers. In addition, employers involved in financing higher education would do whatever they could to ensure that loans or sponsorships received an appropriate return.

Without being unduly optimistic, therefore, a selective system of higher education may provide a platform for the kind of customer-driven, employer-responsive approach the current system is lacking. Moreover, as students' contributions to the cost of higher education come into play, a promising future for higher education could lie ahead. Once universities are allowed to charge their own fees for their degree programmes and adjust the course content to the needs of their customers, then high-quality courses can be priced at a rate which could more than compensate for a temporary loss of earnings, both for students and universities. The proposed system would thus be characterised by

- a 'natural' reduction in student numbers in higher education by means of selection;
- private sector involvement and finance; and
- a purpose-driven approach which will benefit students, employers and the economy as a whole.

The new system would allow students to acquire the skills required by employers; underemployment of graduates would thus be reduced. It would allow the private sector to contribute to a system that introduces flexibility, combats skill shortages and reduces recruitment difficulties. This contribution could take the form of loans, sponsorships or even the finance of specific research projects. At the aggregate level, the proposed system would lead to an economy equipped with motivated and highly skilled young individuals willing to invest in their employment future and ready to face the challenge of ongoing technological change.

9 | Lord Dearing's Response

In July 1997 a proposal for a 'new compact' between the main stakeholders in higher education was put forward by the National Committee of Enquiry into Higher Education (1997), established in May 1996 by agreement between the main political parties and chaired by Sir Ron (now Lord) Dearing. Some of the key principles to which the Committee was asked to have regard include the objective of maximum participation in initial higher education by young and mature students, fair and transparent arrangements for student support, and the achievement of value for money and cost-effectiveness. A number of recommendations were made, including proposals on general funding requirements, lifelong career guidance services, teaching quality assessments and accredited teacher training. The most talked-about recommendation, however, concerned students' contribution to the cost of higher education.

The National Committee's preference was to recommend a system of student payment under which all graduates make a flat-rate contribution of about 25 per cent of average tuition costs, equivalent to about £1,000 per year, at the time of study or by repaying a loan on an income-contingent basis once in employment. The new measures apply to new university entrants in October 1998 and were made against the background that the anticipated further expansion of higher education could not be afforded on the basis of current funding arrangements.[29] Certainly, the introduction of such a system will go some way towards addressing the (funding) crisis in higher education. But will it go far enough?

Although future cohorts of students will be required to pay for their tuition, the proposed system suffers from a number of

---

[29] It has been estimated that a possible increase to 45 per cent full-time participation by young people would lead to a funding gap in 20 years time, amounting to about £2 billion or more (DfEE, 1997).

shortcomings. It is difficult to understand why the proposal does not allow the proportion of tuition costs to be increased without an independent review and a resolution in both Houses of Parliament. Such procedures are lengthy and cumbersome and lack the desired flexibility of a truly reformed system of higher education. In any case, in view of our discussions here, a flat rate of 25 per cent seems to be a rather modest amount. The suggested proportion might have been sufficient in 1963 when Lord Robbins published his review of higher education and when participation rates hovered around the 5 per cent mark. At present, however, it is nowhere near the contribution that would help overcome the funding crisis in higher education, bearing in mind that a mass system of higher education needs to be financed with participation rates of 30 per cent and above. It is hardly surprising, therefore, that some Australian commentators, based on their own experiences of student funding contributions, suggest an increase to around 40 per cent of average tuition costs (Edwards, 1997).

The report does not rule out completely different levels of fees being charged by universities, but makes such developments subject to a number of conditions, including that extra fee charging is not widespread. The Committee thus denied universities the opportunity to open up higher education to real competition which may lead to appropriate quantities and improved qualities of degree courses and respective graduates. Instead, the report encourages the growth of student numbers by suggesting questionable discounts, fees being waived for part-timers, vouchers being offered to help cover tuition costs, and relatively low interest rates for student loans. The report also suggests that government plans to sell student loans to the private sector 'may well represent poor value for money'. It is rather ironic, however, that such remarks come at a time when the taxpayer bears the burden of about £1.7 billion towards students' living costs – nearly 25 per cent of the higher education budget! All that seems to matter to the proposals' advocates is the ultimate aim to widen student access to higher education – a scenario which is hailed by some commentators as 'a triumph of the welfare state' (Barr and Crawford, 1997). Accordingly, little is said about the danger that more students will lower the relative value of university degrees and that low interest rates on student loans may actually provide an incentive for well-off students and their parents to take out the maximum amount allowed, deposit the money in a high-interest account and make a profit on the interest differential. Higher education, *quo vadis*?

10 | The Future of Higher Education in Britain

Promises by politicians to boost education in Britain are in fashion. It is argued that education and training combat the allegedly widespread skill shortages and will lead to better employment prospects for individuals. The Conservative opposition praises itself for its record while in government in delivering education and questions whether the new government will ever measure up to its achievements; the Liberal Democrats are prepared to raise taxation for better schooling and, according to prime minister Tony Blair, the Labour party is still putting three issues at the top of the political agenda: education, education and education. However, across all political parties a number of commentators have found themselves in an equity-efficiency quandary, which has become of increasing concern to governments as public pressure for more education has come into conflict with budgetary pressures.

At the individual level, of course, education and training achievements are extremely valuable assets. Qualifications have never harmed anybody in a society where employment chances are influenced heavily by formal credentials. However, at the macro level things are not so clear-cut. The mystifying assumption that, by improving Britain's education and training record, somehow unemployment will disappear is not just debatable; it is misleading at best, and at worst it is utter nonsense. In Germany, arguably Europe's most successful post-war economy, over 70 per cent of all workers are formally qualified and an increasing number of youngsters enter higher education;[30] yet unemployment is hovering

---

[30] In post-unification Germany there are 318 institutions of higher learning and *Fachhochschulen* (polytechnics, art schools, and music academies) with a total of 1.8 million students. Until the 1960s, 5 per cent of the 18-

around the 4 million mark (Lange and Maguire, 1996). The emphasis on formal qualifications alone without incorporating labour demand may thus lead to the bizarre situation where – like Germany – one ends up with probably the best qualified unemployed workforce in Europe.

It was argued earlier that the key to a successful transition in further and higher education lies in the ability to provide 'high-quality products'. The alternative would be to approve of a mass system at the advanced end of the educational ladder and to interpret such a move as a way of 'expanding business' – access to further and higher education for everybody, low academic standards combined with a lack of vocational values. The student would be a low-quality customer. However, it cannot be in the interest of anybody to pretend that a lowering of academic standards would have no serious effects on the British economy. Academic standards have to meet the requirements which justify the labels 'further' and 'higher'. Conversely, both the assurance to provide a system of higher education for an ever-increasing number of youngsters *without compromise* and the failure to provide a selective system of advanced study might be extremely costly for individuals and society as a whole. At a time when a large number of current further education colleges seek university status, increasing levels of graduate unemployment and a waste of human resources at their potentially most productive age might become an unpleasant reality.

The fundamental, though neglected, questions posed by this paper need to dominate discussion of the future of higher education in Britain. Does Britain provide too much higher education, and are the current funding mechanisms fair and efficient? The argument of this paper is that the answer to the first question is likely to be in the affirmative, and to the second, in the negative. The tentative conclusions are that government has been too concerned to raise numbers entering higher education at the expense of its quality, and with no real economic argument to back this expansion. Moreover, the funding mechanisms currently in place undermine equity, because the relatively less well off subsidise the middle classes, and allow students to make important life decisions without regard to economic considerations. But the solution

---

21-year-old age group were students; today, it is between 25 and 30 per cent (Konow, 1996).

has been implied throughout. Income-contingent loans for students, combined with realistic tuition fees charged by universities, can bring market mechanisms to bear. Through these market mechanisms, desirable changes (some of which we cannot foresee, given the unpredictability of future developments, particularly in technological innovation) will be allowed to occur in higher education. Income-contingent loans allow for repayments without an excessive financial burden, yet incorporate a strong signal which will make students think twice about costs and benefits before entering any particular degree course. And if universities are allowed to charge their own fees, students will vote with their feet and only quality degree programmes will survive in the long run.

References

Albrecht, J.W. (1981): 'A Procedure for Testing the Signalling Hypothesis', *Journal of Public Economics*, Vol. 15, pp. 123-32.

Arrow, K. (1973): 'Higher Education as a Filter', *Journal of Public Economics*, Vol. 2, pp. 193-216.

Ash, M.G. (1996): 'Common and Disparate Dilemmas of German and American Universities', in Muller, S. (ed.), *Universities in the Twenty-First Century*, International Political Currents, Vol. 2, Oxford: Berghahn Books.

Barr, N. (1991): 'Income-Contingent Loans: An Idea Whose Time Has Come', in Shaw, G. K. (ed.), *Economics, Culture and Education: Essays in Honour of Mark Blaug*, Aldershot: Edward Elgar Publishing.

— (1993): 'Alternative Funding Resources for Higher Education', *The Economic Journal*, Vol. 103, No. 418, pp. 718-28, May.

Barr, N. and Falkingham, J. (1993): *Paying for Learning*, Welfare State Programme Working Paper Series WSP/94, London School of Economics, September.

Barr, N. and Crawford, I. (1997): 'A Better Class of Students', *The Guardian Higher Educational Supplement*, 9 September, p.iii.

Bennett, R., Glennerster, H. and Nevison, D. (1992): 'Investing in Skill: To Stay On or Not To Stay On', *Oxford Review of Economic Policy*, Vol. 8, No. 2, pp. 130-45.

Berger, M. and Leigh, P. (1989): 'Schooling, Self-selection and Health', *Journal of Human Resources*, Vol. 24, pp. 433-55.

Blaug, M. (1982): 'The Distributional Effect of Higher Education Subsidies', *Economics of Education Review*, Vol. 2, No. 3, pp. 201-31.

— (1985): 'Where Are We Now in the Economics of Education?', *Economics of Education Review*, Vol. 4, pp. 17-28.

Blundell, R., Dearden, L., Goodman, A. and Reed, H., (1997): *Higher Education, Employment and Earnings in Britain*, London: Institute for Fiscal Studies.

Bowles, S. and Gintis, H. (1975): 'The Problem with Human Capital Theory: A Marxian Critique', *American Economic Review*, Vol. 65, pp. 74-82.

Bowman, M.-J., Millot, B., and Schiefelbein, E. (1984): *The Political Economy of Public Support of Higher Education: Studies in Chile, France and Malaysia*, Washington D.C.: World Bank, Education Department.

British Broadcasting Corporation (1996): 'More Money for Higher Education?', BBC Radio 4, Analysis, November.

Buchanan, J. and Tullock, G. (1962): *The Calculus of Consent*, Ann Arbor, Michigan: University of Michigan Press.

Buchanan, J. et al. (1980): *Toward a Theory of the Rent-seeking Society*, College Station, Texas: Texas A & M Press.

Chapman, B. (1992): *Austudy: Towards a More Flexible Approach*, Canberra: AGPS.

Christoffersen, M.N. (1996): 'Social Consequences of Unemployment', paper presented at the International Labour Markets Conference 1996 on 'Unemployment in Theory and Practice', The Robert Gordon University, Aberdeen, June.

Cochrane, S., O'Hara, D. and Leslie, J. (1980): 'The Effects of Education on Health', *World Bank Staff Working Paper*, No. 405.

Deakin, B. M. (1996): *The Youth Labour Market in Britain: The Role of Intervention*, Cambridge: Cambridge University Press.

Department of Employment (1993): *Education Statistics for the UK*, London: HMSO.

DfEE (Department for Education and Employment) (1997): *Higher Education for the 21st Century: Change in Higher Education*, DfEE WebPages.

Dore, R. (1976): *The Diploma Disease*, London: George Unwin.

Downs, A. (1957): *An Economic Theory of Democracy*, New York: Harper and Row.

Edwards, M. (1997): 'The wonderful wizardry of Oz', *The Guardian Higher Education Supplement*, 9 September, p. ii.

Ellison, R., Tinsley, K., and Houston, N. (1997): 'British Labour Force Projections: 1997-2006', *Labour Market Trends*, February, pp. 51-67.

Fields, G. (1974): 'Private Returns and Social Equity in the Financing of Higher Education', in D. Court and D.P. Ghai (eds.), *Education, Society and Development*, Oxford: Oxford University Press.

Greenaway, D. and Tuck, J. (1995): *Economic Impact of International Students in UK Higher Education*, report prepared for the CVCP, University of Nottingham.

Griliches, Z. and Mason, W.M. (1972): 'Education, Income, and Ability', *Journal of Political Economy*, May-June, pp. 74-103.

Hansen, W. L. and Weisbrod, B.A. (1969): *Benefits, Costs and Finance of Public Higher Education*, Chicago: Markham Publishing.

Hamilton, G. and Roesner, J.D. (1972): 'How Employers Screen Disadvantaged Job Applicants', *Monthly Labor Review*, September.

Higher Education Statistics Agency (1996): *First Destination of Students Leaving Higher Education Institutions 1994/95*, Data Report and Reference Volume, London.

Institute for Employment Studies (1996): *What Do Graduates Really Do?*, Report, Brighton: IES.

Jallade, J.-P. (1973): *The Financing of Education: An Examination of Basic Issues*, World Bank Staff Working Paper No. 157, Washington, D.C.

Kash, D.E. (1990): 'The Future of Higher Education', public lecture at the University of Arizona, mimeo.

Kingston, P. (1997): 'The Clearing Merry-Go-Round has Spare Places. What Went Wrong?', *The Guardian Educational Supplement*, 9 September, p. ii-iii.

Konow, G. (1996): 'Planning, Financing and Accountability of German Universities: Structural and Technical Issues', in S. Muller (ed.), *Universities in the Twenty-First Century*, International Political Currents, Vol. 2, Oxford: Berghahn Books.

La Valle, I., Jagger, N., Connor, H. and Rawlinson, S. (1996): *The IES Annual Graduate Review 1996-1997*, Report 324, Brighton: IES.

Lange, T. and Maguire, K. (1996): 'Dreaming of a Britain Like Germany', *Economic Affairs*, Vol. 16, No. 5, pp. 39-41, London: Institute of Economic Affairs.

Lissenburgh, S. and A. Bryson (1996): *The Returns to Graduation*, London: Policy Studies Institute.

Lucas, R. (1988): 'On the Mechanics of Economic Development', *Journal of Monetary Economics*, Vol. 22, pp. 3-42.

Mason, G. (1997): 'Learning for Labour', *The Guardian Higher Education Supplement*, 18 February.

McClelland, C. (1980): *State, Society and University in Germany 1700-1914*, Cambridge: Cambridge University Press.

Meesook, O.A. (1984): *Financing and Equity in the Social Sciences in Indonesia*, World Bank Staff Working Paper No. 703, Washington D.C.

Morris, M. (1989): 'Student Aid in Sweden: Recent Experience and Reforms', in M. Woodhall (ed.), *Financial Support for Students: Grants, Loans or Graduate Tax?*, London: Kogan Page.

National Committee of Inquiry into Higher Education (1997): *Higher Education in the Learning Society*, Summary Report, July.

Orivel, F. (1996): 'The State of Research in Economics Education: A General Overview and the French Situation', in D. Benner and D. Lenzen (eds.), *Education for the New Europe*, Oxford: Berghahn Books.

Peacock, Alan T. and Wiseman, Jack (1964): *Education for Democrats*, Hobart Paper 25, London: Institute of Economic Affairs.

Pearson, R. et al. (1989): *How Many Graduates in the 21st Century? The Choice is Yours*, Report No. 177, Brighton: IMS.

Pechman, J.A. (1970): 'The Distributional Effect of Public Higher Education in California', *Journal of Human Resources*, Vol. 5, No. 3, pp. 361-70.

Phelps, E.S. (1972): 'The Statistical Theory of Racism and Sexism', *American Economic Review*, September.

PIP (Performance Indicator Project) (1996): *Signposts to Employability: Graduate Recruiters' Survey 1996*, Lincolnshire: PIP.

Psacharopoulos, G. (1973): *Returns to Education: An International Comparison*, Amsterdam and New York: Elsevier.

— (1977): 'The Perverse Effect of Public Subsidisation of Education', *Comparative Education Review*, Vol. 21, No. 1, pp. 69-90.

— (1981): 'Returns to Education: An Updated International Comparison', *Comparative Education*, Vol. 17, No. 3, pp. 321-41.

— (1987): 'To Vocationalize or Not To Vocationalize? That Is The Curriculum Question', *International Review of Education*, Vol. XXXIII, pp. 187-211.

Psacharopoulos, G. and Woodhall, M. (1991): *Education for Development: An Analysis of Investment Choices*, Oxford: Oxford University Press.

PSI (1991): *Britain in 2010*, London: Policy Studies Institute.

Rawlinson, S., Frost, D. and Walsh, K. (1996): *The FE/HE Interface: A UK Perspective*, Report 316, Brighton: IES.

Rice, L.D. (1977): *Student Loans: Problems and Policy Alternatives*, New York: College Entrance Examination Board.

Riley, J. (1979): 'Testing the Educational Screening Hypothesis', *Journal of Political Economy*, Vol. 87, pp. 227-52.

Rosenzweig, M. (1990): 'Population Growth and Human Capital Investments', *Journal of Political Economy*, Vol. 98, pp. 538-70.

Schultz, T.W. (1972): 'Optimal investment in college instruction: equity and efficiency', *Journal of Political Economy*, Vol. 80, pp. 1-23.

Seville, A., and Tooley, J. (1997): *The Debate on Higher Education*, IEA Studies in Education No. 5, London: Institute of Economic Affairs.

Siebert, W.S. (1985): 'Developments in the Economics of Human Capital', in Carline, D., Pissarides, C.A., Siebert, W.S. and Sloane, P.J. (eds.), *Surveys in Economics: Labour Economics*, Longman: London and New York.

Siegel, I.H. (1967): 'On Manpower, Forecasting, and Public-Private Roles: Three Evolving Concepts', in Siegel, I.H. (ed.), *Manpower Tomorrow: Prospects and Priorities*, New York: Augustus M. Kelley Publishers.

Skills and Enterprise Network (1997): *Labour Market Quarterly Report*, February.

Spence, M.A. (1973): 'Job Market Signalling', *Quarterly Journal of Economics*, Vol. 87, pp. 355-75.

Stigler, G.J. (1971): 'The Theory of Economic Regulation', *Bell Journal of Economics*, Vol.2, No. 1.

Stiglitz, J. (1975): 'The Theory of Screening, Education and the Distribution of Income', *American Economic Review*, June, pp. 283-300.

Sperling, J. and Tucker, R.W., (1997): *For-Profit Higher Education: developing a world-class workforce*, New Brunswick and London: Transaction Publishers.

Sperling, J. (1998): 'The American For-Profit University', *Economic Affairs*, Vol. 18, No. 3.

Taubman, P.J. and Wales, T.J. (1974): *Education and Earnings: College as an Investment and Screening Device*, New York: McGraw-Hill.

Tooley, J. (1996): 'Qualification Inflation', *Economic Affairs*, Vol. 16, No. 5, p. 49, London: Institute of Economic Affairs.

Weale, M. (1992): 'Education, Externalities, Fertility and Economic Growth', paper presented to the ESRC Economics of Education Study Group, November.

— (1993): 'A Critical Evaluation of Rate of Return Analysis', *Economic Journal*, Vol. 103, No. 418, pp. 729-37.

West, E.G. (1994): *Britain's Student Loan System in World Perspective: A Critique*, Current Controversies No. 9, London: Institute of Economic Affairs.

— (1995): 'The Economics of Higher Education', in J. W. Sommer (ed.), *The Academy in Crisis: the political economy of higher education*, Oakland, California: The Independent Institute.

— (1998): 'The Role of Income Tax in Student Loan Repayments', *Economic Affairs*, Vol. 18, No. 3.

Woodhall, M. (1982): *Student Loans: Lessons from Recent International Experiences*, London: Policy Studies Institute.

The Debate on Higher Education

Challenging the Assumptions

Higher education in the UK is at a crucial juncture in its history. Its funding is in crisis, and morale amongst students and academics perilously low. This monograph offers two contributions to the debate.

Like many of the nationalised industries of old, producer-driven higher education suffers from inefficiencies and lack of responsiveness to its consumers: Adrian Seville shows how modularisation – the introduction of 'quasi'-markets in higher education – could ameliorate some of these problems.

His paper explores fundamental issues, and challenges whether the current quality control mechanisms in higher education can be considered satisfactory even in a traditional university setting, let alone when modularisation is introduced.

Tooley's contribution takes the debate a step further. The suggestion of 'quasi'-markets in higher education begs the question as to why not 'genuine' markets? Hence he examines the fundamental assumption which remains unchallenged in much of the current debate: why should government be involved in higher education at all? He looks at the major justifications given for government intervention, and finds each wanting.

Government is not needed to make higher education opportunities available. Indeed, there are negative effects of such intervention, including qualification inflation. Finally, the desirable goal of equity in terms of access to higher learning only needs the minimal intervention of private income-contingent loans for tuition and maintenance, not the gamut of interference with which we are familiar.

The Institute of Economic Affairs
2 Lord North Street, Westminster, London SW1P 3LB
Telephone: 0171 799 3745 Facsimile: 0171 799 2137
E-mail: iea@iea.org.uk Internet: http://www.iea.org.uk

£10.00

ISBN 0-255 36409-1

The Dilemma of Democracy:

The Political Economics of Over-Government

Arthur Seldon

1. Economists' notions of 'public goods' have provided the intellectual backing for the expansion of government-provided goods and services.
2. Governments have taken control of activities – 'public' goods, 'public utilities', welfare, local government services – which would have been better left to the private sector: they were mostly being privately provided before being crowded out by the state.
3. If government does not withdraw from many of its functions, people will increasingly escape to non-state suppliers. They may also refuse to pay for state activities they regard as superfluous.
4. Government will have to reduce its share of national income from over 40 to nearer 20 per cent.
5. 'Democracy' today generally represents the tyranny of the majority. Organised groups extract favours from government at the expense of those who are unorganised, unschooled or unskilled. Even worse, the people are incited to thwart their long–term interests by snatching short–term gains.
6. Attempts to correct market 'imperfections' create over-government. The '...evidence of history is that the imperfections of government are more deep-rooted and less remediable than the imperfections of the market.' Government 'remedies' begin too soon, go too far and carry on too long.
7. As government has grown too large, people have found means of escape - for example, by the 'parallel economy', by barter to avoid taxes, by electronic money, by the Internet and by taking advantage of liberalised trade and modern communications to use facilities in other countries without moving home.
8. A new mercantilism is emerging as government, to preserve its position, tries to regulate industry and commerce, including labour. But the market, which gives the power of exit, will outlast politicised alternatives.
9. Government must accept that it has lost the power to maintain its economic empire. 'The escapable power of political government..' is up against '...the irresistible economic force of the market.'
10. The remaining decision for government is to '...arrange its retreat with dignity before the escapes multiply to deprive it of the authority to influence the rate of its withdrawal.' Hobbes' warning has been trumped by Spinoza's vision.

The Institute of Economic Affairs

2 Lord North Street, Westminster, London SW1P 3LB
Telephone: 0171 799 3745 Facsimile: 0171 799 2137
Email: iea@iea.org.uk Internet: http://www.iea.org.uk

£10.00

ISBN: 0 255 36417-2

Corporate Governance:
Accountability in the Marketplace

Elaine Sternberg

1. Businesses and corporations are not the same thing: not all corporations are businesses, and most businesses are not corporations. Whereas 'business' designates a particular objective, 'corporation' designates a particular organisational structure.
2. Corporate governance refers to ways of ensuring that corporate actions, assets and agents are directed at achieving the corporate objectives established by the corporation's shareholders (as set out in the Memorandum of Association or comparable constitutional document).
3. Many criticisms of corporate governance are based on false assumptions about what constitutes ethical conduct by corporations, and confusions about what corporate governance is.
4. Protests against takeovers, 'short-termism', redundancies and high executive remuneration are typically objections to specific corporate outcomes, not criticisms of corporate governance.
5. Many misguided criticisms of the Anglo-Saxon model come from confusing corporate governance with government: it is a mistake to criticise corporations for not achieving public policy objectives, and for not giving their stakeholders the rights and privileges commonly associated with citizenship.
6. Some criticisms of the traditional Anglo-Saxon model of corporate governance are justified. There are serious practical obstacles that prevent shareholders from keeping their corporations and corporate agents properly accountable.
7. Though commonly praised, the German and Japanese systems are considerably less capable of achieving the definitive purpose of corporate governance than the Anglo-Saxon model is. Neither is designed to protect, nor typically used for protecting, property rights.
8. The increasingly popular stakeholder theory is also incapable of providing better corporate governance. Stakeholder theory is incompatible with all substantial objectives and undermines both private property and accountability.
9. Regulation that attempts to improve corporate governance by limiting shareholders' options, and reducing their freedom to control their own companies as they choose, is necessarily counterproductive.
10. The way to respond to flaws in current Anglo-Saxon corporate governance mechanisms is to improve the accountability of corporations to their ultimate owners, preferably by having corporations compete for investment, and institutional investors for funds, in part on the degree of accountability they offer to their beneficial owners.

The Institute of Economic Affairs
2 Lord North Street, Westminster, London SW1P 3LB
Telephone: 0171 799 3745   Facsimile: 0171 799 2137
E-mail: iea@iea.org.uk   Internet: http://www.iea.org.uk

£12.00

ISBN 0-255 36416-4

Regulating Utilities: Understanding the Issues

Utility regulation in Britain has now entered a phase in which debate is no longer so much concerned with whether it is preferable to rival systems but with how to shape the 'regulatory contract' in monopoly areas and, in potentially competitive areas, how to ensure rivalry.

The latest version of this annual volume of Readings, published jointly by the Institute and London Business School, contains papers by eminent commentators on utility regulation and comments by the regulators themselves.

Contents

Introduction
M.E. BEESLEY

- Regulatory Institutions and Regulatory Policy for Economies in Transition
  MARTIN CAVE AND JON STERN, Comments by SIR BRYAN CARSBERG
- Local Competition in UK Telecommunications
  MARK ARMSTRONG, Comments by M.E. BEESLEY
- Progress in Gas Competition
  GEORGE YARROW, Comments by EILEEN MARSHALL
- Regulatory Asset Value and the Cost of Capital
  GEOFFREY WHITTINGTON, Comments by IAN BYATT
- Pool Reform and Competition in Electricity
  DAVID NEWBERY, Comments by STEPHEN LITTLECHILD,
  Additional Comments by GEOFFREY HORTON
- When is Discrimination Undue?
  JOHN VICKERS, Comments by JOHN BRIDGEMAN
- MMC and Decisions on RPI-x
  MARTIN HOWE, Comments by COLIN ROBINSON
- What Next in UK Railways?
  JOHN WELSBY, Comments by CHRIS BOLT

The Institute of Economic Affairs
2 Lord North Street, Westminster, London SW1P 3LB
Telephone: 0171 799 3745 Facsimile: 0171 799 2137
E-mail: iea@iea.org.uk Internet: http://www.iea.org.uk

£17.00

ISBN 0-255 36418-0

The Changing Fortunes of Economic Liberalism
Yesterday, Today and Tomorrow

David Henderson

1. Liberalism implies '...restricting the powers and functions of governments, so as to give full scope for individuals, families and enterprises.' But the state has an important role in '...establishing and maintaining a framework in which markets can function effectively...'

2. The doctrine of economic liberalism goes back about two and a half centuries. Over that period there has been no consistent trend towards liberal economic policies: indeed, liberalism was generally in decline over the hundred years up to the late 1970s.

3. But in the last two decades many governments have adopted reform programmes which have liberalised their economies and international transactions have been freed. The Economic Freedom of the World project, for example, shows a clear trend towards liberalisation in many countries - especially since 1985.

4. Few, if any, countries which have embarked on economic reform in the last twenty years have consciously reversed direction. The improvement in the fortunes of economic liberalism seems more than an 'accident of fashion'.

5. Reforming governments have appeared in every region of the world and from both the 'left' and the 'right' of the conventional political spectrum. They have included authoritarian regimes though there is a strong association between political and economic freedoms.

6. It is not true that coalitions of interests largely preclude economic liberalisation otherwise, the reforms of recent years would not have taken place.

7. Liberal ideas have regained ground within the economics profession after a period from the 1930s to the 1970s when they were regarded as 'less central' than previously.

8. The 'balance of informed opinion' has also shifted to embrace liberal ideas. Politicians, civil servants and central bankers all came to support structural economic reforms from the mid-1980s onwards - even before the collapse of communism powerfully reinforced the liberal cause.

9. Despite the spread of liberal ideas, liberalism has a 'chronic weakness' because its conscious adherents are so few. In most countries majority opinion remains hostile to 'leaving it to the market', partly because of the continuing hold of pre-economic ideas.

10. Although events and continuing technical progress will probably continue to favour the liberal cause, anti-liberal ideas are still strong. Extending market reforms into areas so far untouched by liberalisation will be difficult. Hence the fortunes of economic liberalism in the early twenty first century are 'clouded and in doubt'.

The Institute of Economic Affairs
2 Lord North Street, Westminster, London SW1P 3LB
Telephone: 0171 799 3745 Facsimile: 0171 799 2137
E-mail: iea@iea.org.uk Internet: http://www.iea.org.uk

£12.00

ISBN 0-255 36419-9